D0359884

# Orangutan Baby

by Monica Hughes

**Consultant: Mitch Cronick**

# BEARPORT
PUBLISHING COMPANY, INC.
New York, New York

# Credits

All images courtesy of Digital Vision

Library of Congress Cataloging-in-Publication Data

Hughes, Monica.

Orangutan baby / by Monica Hughes.

p. cm. — (I love reading)

Includes bibliographical references and index.

ISBN 1-59716-153-5 (library binding : alk. paper) — ISBN 1-59716-179-9 (pbk. : alk. paper)

1. Orangutan — Infancy — Juvenile literature. I. Title. II. Series.

QL737.P96H84 2006

599.88'3139 — dc22

2005030829

For more information, write to Bearport Publishing Company, Inc., 101 Fifth Avenue, Suite 6R, New York, New York 10003. Printed in the United States of America.

1 2 3 4 5 6 7 8 9 10

The I Love Reading series was originally developed by Tick Tock Media.

# CONTENTS

# What is an orangutan?

An orangutan is a big **ape**.

Orangutan

Orangutans live in **rain forests.**

They live high up in the trees.

# What does an orangutan look like?

An orangutan has long, orange hair.

An orangutan has long arms.

Father orangutans are very big.

7

# Meet a baby orangutan

This is a baby orangutan with his mother.

Baby orangutans live with their mothers.

They do not live with their fathers.

9

# What does the baby orangutan eat?

The baby orangutan eats fruit.

His mother chews the fruit to make it soft.

Then she gives it to her baby.

The baby drinks his mother's milk, too.

# When does the baby get his own food?

When the baby is bigger, he gets his own food.

He eats fruit and leaves.

He eats **ants**, **snails**, and eggs, too.

# How does the baby get around?

The mother orangutan has long hair.

The baby holds on to her long hair when she swings from tree to tree.

# Where does the baby sleep?

The baby orangutan sleeps with his mother at night.

His mother uses leaves to make a **nest** high up in the trees.

She makes a new nest every night.

# When does the baby live on his own?

When the baby gets bigger,
he lives on his own.

He holds on to the branches.

He swings from tree to tree.

# Why are orangutans in danger?

Orangutans make their homes in trees.

The trees in a rain forest can be cut down.

If all the trees are cut down, the orangutans will have no place to live.

# Glossary

**ants** (ANTS) small insects that live in big groups

**ape** (APE) an animal that looks like a monkey but has no tail; orangutans and chimpanzees are some kinds of apes

**Chimpanzee**

**nest** (NEST) an animal bed

**rain forests** (RAYN FOR-ists) warm, damp places with lots of trees

**snails** (SNAYLZ) small animals that have soft bodies usually covered with a shell

# Index

# Learn More

**Eckart, Edana.** *Orangutan.* Danbury, CT: Children's Press (2003).

**Ring, Susan.** *Project Orangutan.* New York: Weigl Educational Publishers (2003).

www.animaland.org/asp/encyclopedia/orangutan.asp

www.nationalgeographic.com/kids/creature_feature/0102/orangutans.html